PAPER SHADOWS

JEMMA LOUISE LIDGARD

Copyright © Jemma L Lidgard

The right of Jemma L Lidgard to be identified as the author of this work has been asserted by the author in accordance with the Copyright, Designs and Patents Act 1988.

All rights reserved.

No part of this publication may be reproduced or transmitted in any form or by any means, electronic or mechanical, including photocopy, recording or any information storage and retrieval system, without permission in writing from the author or publisher.

ISBN: 978 1 836 54369 5

Cover design Michael Stephenson
Editor and typesetter Helen Jones

Acknowledgements

To my family and friends, and to those who brought me out of the shadows and revealed their true characters.

PAPER SHADOWS

Contents

Introduction

1. Expedition   7
(nature, exploration, climate change)

2. Emotional Struggles   19
(anxiety, uncertainty, loss, betrayal, loneliness and rejection)

3. Escapism   44
(intoxication, fantasy)

4. Resilience and Recovery   58
(survival, strength, self-love, healing)

5. Cosmic and Existential Reflections   83
(celestial, universe, existentialism, mortality)

6. Human Connections   108
(lust, infatuation, modern life)

7. The Darkest Hours   133
At night-time, the darkness awakens our most intrusive and irrational thoughts

Introduction

The stages of writing start from pen to paper, fingertips to keyboard, scribbling out the mistakes, backspacing the pain with the delete button, revealing taboos. The vulnerabilities that we store are now out of the shadows – an unrequited conversation that we can trust only with ourselves. Never feeling good enough, feeling frustrated or misunderstood, there is a festering silence that moulds a silhouette. Shadows form all our connections and dreams, as well as those shattered by the human experiences of loss, rejection, loneliness, and death.

This is what it is to 'be'. Above the surface, breathing and floating as the light refracts onto the water currents. A reminder that the shadows can disappear whilst we exist as our organic and unfinished selves in an already broken, fast-paced modern world, with so many fragments to piece together and experiences still to be told. The shadows are projections of our realities blocked by the light source, that simply cast a feeling. But they can be stepped on and nobody would feel a thing. Poetry is a shadow.

1. Expedition
(nature, exploration, climate change)

Decomposition

Mountains are a collision between the mind and body
Sheared stress under these conditions
Sloping sides and rounded fists
Grab onto those rocks that keep you amidst
Wind and rain pummel the body
Battered down in vain
Fractured ego and erosion
Pools of sweat drip into the ridges of your bones
Anatomy carved by glaciers and streams
Separated by the valleys that flow through the cracks in your palms
Trapped within the pores of your skin
A thickened crust of mud and shit
Boots crunch into the folds of the rugged landscape
Soiled into the earth as it rotates
Rebirth

1. EXPEDITION

Beachcomber

Glencoe wanderer
Wavering around the windy road
A break in the heat at the Green Welly Stop
Kitsch fridge magnets and food for the hearty
Kilted dogs for the lonely hiker
Flowing dams that trickle into the bloodstream
Purifying scream of delight
Cooling down in Scottish fever
En route to the rugged West Coast
To kayak the northern sea and float to Eigg
Past yachts and boats
Refrain from a reality that boasts and gloats
Jellyfish are your friends
Mineral salty sea-green
Swept up in breezeless currents
Blue buoyance

Geese

Flight over frozen land
Migrate in the winter to warmer grounds
Further away to nest
Adjoining fields disconnected through distance
The ice remains solid in a thawing flock
Wings shaped to shelter
A search for soft, spongy marshland
Graze and rest

1. EXPEDITION

Voyage

Salmon skies
A dish made for angel delight
Pink stodgy sludge of frothy waves
Seabirds waddle on gunky ground
As the metal detector transforms into a corroded
    demon
Removes razor throats and chokes on silver spoons
For the fish-limbed creature
Adds rust to the toxic treasure trove
Of underwater secrets, bespoke and unbroken
The voice of a screeching siren
An aquatic emergency
Pollution

Anticipation

A muddy brown stream rushes through crevices
Frothy cola fizzes into sensations of blissful bubbles
Disguised by the ticks that bury themselves under your skin
Feeding, blood-sucking pests
Lyme disease falls from every sedimentary rock
Picking and scratching until it scars the landscape of every flowing stream
The tap is too tight to stop the liquid from gushing
Out of control in weathered hands and flimsy nails
A moment of overflow
Bursting at the seams
Cleansed

1. EXPEDITION

Inauguration

Royal orange burnt flame ball
In the midnight sky
Of wispy clouds
The only beacon of hope
In cloaked darkness
Over thoughts and feelings
The emptiness is filled with a fruitful peach
To bring health and sunshine
As you stretch to early skies
A new day begins
Succulent creation

New season

Spring rises out of the dampened slime
Better weather and blossomed trees
But my body is still a season behind

1. EXPEDITION

Downpour

All it ever does is rain
Perhaps this is nature's cry for help
Distressed, war-torn landscape walked with pain
Sensitive to our footprints, each vein and fibre is linked
    to the underground habitat
Fungal networks communicate with fine roots to and
    from our brains
It is a signal to repair all the damage humans have
    inflicted in 'vain'
As you sigh, there is anger in the air
A suppressed scream carried through the breeze
Inhaled torture soaking into the leaves
Rushing through the stems to provide nutrients in the
    ground
It can't be excused for another season; it is more than
    just a 'feeling'
Earth-bound trauma

Summer solstice

On the evening of the first summer in the northern hemisphere
Warm, stuffy air encircles a ring of dancers around a fire pit
Chanting hand-in-hand in floating white gowns and flower crowns
Solar energy soaked between sunset and sea
This pagan event will bring light and vitality in the darkest of times
And when the night draws in, make a wish and dispose of those crowns
Sailing away under moonshine in twilight hours
Temporal royalty crowned the seals and jellyfish
Curious to see, entangled in ribbons and plastic roses
To celebrate our seasonal cycles, we must protect the life cycles of marine creatures
Engulfed in a selfish, celebratory consumption

1. EXPEDITION

Seascape

The DESIRE to inhale. Exhale. Visualise. Feel. Touch. Your breath is escapable, capturing every essence of fresh, sea air.

A sigh of relief and momentary alleviation is absorbed into the blood of the body, flowing to the brain in increasing stimulation. While the lungs are filtered. Filtered with bittersweet surroundings, and scents of nostalgia and unfamiliarity.

It is hot. SUNLIGHT seeps through the Perspex of blue. Blue is the colour of calmness and tranquillity beyond the realm of visual perspectives. Colour is the form of the mind and results in sensorial and visual organisations. They are languages that combine emotions with familiarity such as the heat and sun relating to orange or yellow. HEAT rays absorb, absorb, absorb until the body becomes fatigued. Exhausted and restless, the sun is a mechanism of deflagration. Physically and mentally, abusing your feeling of comfort; dripping with sweat, quenching your thirst and your irritable behaviour is revealed. The desire to unwind can be underestimated by the power of nature, such force strong enough to interrupt the beauty and repose of a 'vacation'. The sand crystallises beneath the cracks in your toes. Heat worsens, unbearable to place any flesh against the grains, you are grounded in your own imprisonment.

MELANCHOLIA of vicious waves roll into one another, racing spontaneously to the finish line. FROTHING into bubbly gestures, broken down by humans and children's laughter that impulse a harmony between them. The gallant crashing of the waves becomes a work of art itself, a symphony, or a band perhaps – besides the seagulls' repetitive vocals that compete. Seascape becomes a formation of sound.

SURFERS weave inside the mystical spray as if a sewing machine needle was piercing through fabric. Some of them triumph in the great bounds of salty twists, but some of them fail and all that's left is a neglected surfboard pulsating into the Perspex of blue. The sea is a mysterious coven into adventures waiting to evolve, although it is dangerous and a threat beneath the continuous leaps and rolls of joy; a beauty that brings happiness and admiration, is also illusory. It is seen as an illusion of desire, but a place where deceit and destruction begin.

2. *Emotional Struggles*
(anxiety, uncertainty, loss, betrayal, loneliness and rejection)

Exile

I gave you my soul every time I fucked you
Your body was my homeland
Beneath the unearthed scars
Feelings don't fade away
Brush all the pain under the rug
Until it becomes dusty love
Relinquish your existence
Ex-land
Distant memory
Let it all go

Seasick

My mum said that the sea can make you sick
She said if you are on a rocking boat
Going from side to side, up and down
You will be throwing up your ice cream float

My mum said that it would be a choppy ride
If it is a windy day, waves will bash into the boat
Sea levels will rise
And you need to time it right with the tide
I am just along for the ride anyway

My mum said to hold on tight to the rails
Or your knees will quake, and your body will shake
Too late for that
I have already gone off the rails

My mum said if you look too far over the edge
You will go overboard
In fact, it is Steve that sent me over the edge
I am sick to death of Steve
Seasick Steve

Starry night

Feel the fury and forced misery
In the screeching, spiralling, deceitful sparkles
That illuminate the oily sky
Like a Van Gogh painting
And with every prying eye
Each mark creates an impression

Curdling and concentric halos
Fizzle into spots of wicked sins
Dispersing into trails of breathless fog
Fear, let the body snatchers win
Seep into the air and through the vents of drains
Absorbing the veins of living souls

Torment
The dog shivers, panting and pacing
Tongue lolling in desperation
Heart racing
And its pupils dilate
Flooding into the artist's palette

Mother of pearl

Pearlescent balls of beauty and grace
Soft flesh and divine value
Coated to protect from the stormy seas
As another clam shuts, another one opens
The world is your oyster

Luscious pearls of pleasure and cultivation
The chain snaps and one by one
Each pearl drops to the floor like pattering rain
Synchronised pain and freedom
No strings attached, loose beads on the run

Trodden into the ground
Fragile porcelain
Of crushed calcium and iridescent curiosity
Tear-drop pearls
Ripple into wounded salty water

Positive

Life is a test
Positive and negative
It doesn't all add up
Until you get the result you want
Small plastic tube with a blue cross
Not a lifesaver
Is it a blessing or a mess?
Decision maker
Your life depends on it

2. EMOTIONAL STRUGGLES

Pink

Looking through rose-coloured lenses
As time passes at quartz two hours
Gone within a purplish blink
Sitting in a blazed magenta shade
Carnation's bloom, perfumy lavender hue
Fragrant feelings fizz into hot pink lemonade
Of crushed strawberries and dreams
Head-fused fuchsia daze
The phase radiates a rosy blush on your cheeks
Turning to a fiery flushed face of Venetian blood
Pink seeps into red
Realism

Blue bench

The loudest bench in the quietest of gardens
Spring blues with blossomed envy
Just waiting for a seater, to soak in all of nature's hues
Reflect and rest in a place of commemoration
For the lonely and wounded souls
Patched by the cherry petals that whisper in the wind
Sitting with your personal therapist
Ventriloquist speaks the wider picture
A spoken silence in one's head
Voice of experience from the wooden dummy
Making space to plan their death

Player

Freshly laid out on the deck
Belgian-Genoese suited for the occasion
Sentimental design of twisted cherubs
The king of hearts waits for his disco queen of clubs
To play her for a fool
The jack of all trades digs the earth with the two of spades
And presents her with eight encrusted diamonds
Offering his winning hand-in-hand
A dealer must play his cards right
Trickery

Wasteland

The earth is bitter cold
Laminated in dry ice
Stamped by frost-bitten toes
That imprint trails of sticky blood

Wounded too much to walk the world
Dangerous territory bordered by lies and thieves
Kidnapping your heart and humility
Discarded and used when they are pleased

As you glaciate into space
You never know how to feel warm again
Frozen and misplaced in cosmic lands
High enough to flee all facades
Glorification

Disappointment

Exhausting and unpleasant
It is a bitter pill to swallow
Fizzle inside like tonic on ice
But you know it will revive
An antiseptic to all the lies

Erasure

Rub out the iris and pupils in their eyes
Scratch out the corneas
So, they become a colourless mediocre sphere
And bury them into the back of your skull
A place for them to rot in the graveyard
As colossal nature intertwines, there is no time to rise from the dead
Ambushed resurrection
Unmemorable misfortune

Consumer

Welcome
Take all that you can get
Replace my voids with decoys and distractions
Until the time ticks and an explosion detonates
Poof into ashes, disappear for your selfish needs
Back to military places
Where is the sacrifice that we plead?
Goodbye to our wasted spaces
And another one bites the dust
In no man's land

Memento mori

Let the ghosts linger in the graveyard
For unsettled rest
You are a dull and fickle soul
That haunts and tricks the lover into love
For they are wise to the old bones that tap on their
   shoulder
They grew stronger and colder
Tears dried out like your dusty ashes in the hourglass
Grim weeper

Cheater

Faster than the sunrise
Speed enough to make the heart race
A cheetah plays by their own rules
Deceived by the snacks received
Spots blot into inky ripped wounds
Dried out in fresh fear
Thirst for juicy prey
Moonlight chasing behind his tail
Disturb the habitat and set a wildfire
As he lies guilty on deserted land
Cheater

Convenience store

Step into glass revolving doors
A world where everything is transparent and free
Glazy daze through the windowpane
Wiping your feet on the mat
Scraping at the shit nesting into your shoes
The last stain of your soul retreats
Worn out and abused

Greedy for all the sweets on the shelves
Spoilt for choice
But before you go, dispose of the wrappers
Bubble gum disease and sugary disposition
Swallowed the chocolate whole
And now you leave as your taste buds are satisfied
With the popping candy in your eyes
That crackle into flames and burn out into flickering
    streetlights
Out of service for another day

Birthday cake

Another year around the sun and nothing has changed
With the early sunrise comes the expectation of
  surprises
Gifts in the shape of kisses from sherried and sugared
  lips
A greedy celebration on your special day
Much older but still unwise
You suck the sickly-sweet icing from your fingertips
Addicted to the jammy and buttercream frosting
The stomach is whipped
Though Victoria's sponge wasn't filling enough
You can't have your cake and eat it too

'Moth-er'

Often misunderstood, they eat the shit out of your furniture and lay eggs on your clothes. They feed and feed until one day your closet will be full of holes, just like the holes in our hearts.

Deadwood

The people grow uglier
Terrorising your brains into games of twister and chess
Trace your limbs on the list
For the players that lose to cheating
And for the ones that don't make a move
The forest of bodies whips and snaps, checkmated by the fool
Collapse on painted spots concealed by mossy peat
Woodland heap

Neutral

Strip back the paper
Apply a chemical solution to all your problems
Clear resin toxins stain the throat and nose
White spirit puddles in lost hope
To mask the musky smell
You can't apply fresh coats of paint
To underlying layers of stale yellow
These uninhabited voids fester mould and decay
Colourless silence is dead air
For all those who suffocate in confined spaces
Solitude

Flamingo

Wings spread to grow
The dress is ruffled
Neon, pink glow
Desired but disappointed

Kitsch aesthetic
Shelf life of five years
Powered by electric
Blood-red feathers

Plaything

Do you ever think about *our* dreams and desires?
How do *we* fit into your life?
A toy to play with until you are bored
Must *we* use all our battery power to be adored?
There is nothing special anymore

Lunch

Empty cafeteria light flickering
No one to drink tea with
Vending machines creaking
Blinkered fridge with mottled milk
A rancid odour

Woven

I just want to be *something*
That melts into the ruffled mess of bed sheets
Creased covers in my wrinkled, wrought hands
Grey to blend in with my ageing hair
Settle down for a lifetime
Invisible blanket

Scavenger

You could be sliding into the open ocean
Musing into blue enormity, unaccompanied in a peaceful fear
A dark whirlpool swallows you in, entangled by the whistles of sirens and fish fins
Jellyfish tentacles asphyxiate the throat, for the unconsciousness to evolve into the subconscious
So, you can exist as a figment rather than a human
No matter where the currents take you, your departure is a shipwreck on the seabed
Wanderlust betrayed

3. *Escapism*
(intoxication, fantasy)

Supermarket

Acid green
Not your usual shopping trip
Broccoli carnations bloom
Advertised through coloured vision

Distorted voice
Cackling through the Tannoy
Enough to annoy anyone

Stumbling over your feet
Strawberry ice
A feeling so nice
Divine taste and a smell so sweet

Fuchsia turns to salmon pink
Something smells rather fishy

Peas roll around
Like green glass marbles
Don't trip

Melted skulls
Crying over the spilt milk
Clotting around your feet

A message in a bottle drift
Through vodka tears

Wiry zigzag floor
Things turned sour
A subconscious war

Cleaning mop on aisle three
Entangled spaghetti sweeps the floor
Splattered minced meat
Splashed into liquid paint

Potatoes with smiley faces
Earth is breathing
A euphoric awakening
Lucid dreaming

3. ESCAPISM

Heinz blood-heads
Soupy mess
Baked beans and bread

Fruit loops
Twisty, bendy strawberry laces
Cashier with his eyes inside out
Check out

Turquoise and red bleeding Aquafresh
Minty squiggles for your breath
Swirling into piped, jammy biscuits
Everything is possible

Lithium

Alkali demon stored in a vacuum
Ready to be unleashed
For potential toxicity
Electrode
Too trembly, vomiting
Dead
No charge, negative battery

3. ESCAPISM

Spell

Tiny tubes of sugar-coated fairy dust, so *they* say, make all your dreams and wishes come true
Intoxicate the body with magical powers – powdered hours
Vanish away your fears, expel your demons, flutter away to folklore and play
For the unearthly experience, cast this spell once a day:

A sprinkle of mummy dust
To induce the abortion
A white pill or two
To reduce the pain
A bottle of alcohol
To induce the regret
A pinch of grounded sea salt
To reduce the anxiety
A cup half empty of coffee
To induce the brain

A stench of fresh air
To reduce the thoughts
A spoonful or two of sugar
To induce the depression
A recipe for disaster
To reduce the mundane

Mischievous and tinkered mind, warped in an enchanting smile
Great Mother in time to repeat the spell and REWIND
Unconditional happiness all bottled up in vial
Hypnotic control, cloak those memories for your immortal soul

Bloody Mary

That bloody Mary
She can't handle a drink
Doesn't quite care
And gets herself into some hot mess

Slurred speech in the mirror
Covered in tomato juice
Not blood, of course
A ritual to reveal the future

That bloody Mary
Popular in the morning
But by noon
She's plotting her next move

Flushed cheeks
Served herself well
And not in a tall glass
As the effects wear off

Bloody Mary isn't my cup of tea
But a preferred cocktail instead
A bit mixed up
She infuriates me

Cinema

Silver screen
Be the hero of your movie
Metallic man
A Hollywood icon for her eyes to see
In all glory, enveloped dreams

Tropical fish flicker through the media stream
Aquamarine blue and fused neon glow
Exotically erotic
In a tank for his view
A watcher is always on time for the show

Glazed gaze
Alter-reality between a mirrored barrier
Observe her soul in between the vivid reef
Two lovers apart
Sealed emotions in an immortalised world of beauty
    and beliefs

Play and repeat
In the cold or the heat
Of a moment that separates fantasy between glass
 fibres
Admiration plays on your infatuated reflection
Closing credits of motion pictures

Yellow

Yell or bellow the colour yellow
Warm and fuzzy feelings
Shine brightly onto dainty buttercups
Melted sugary citrine
Curdled lemon tart crusts and juicy zest
Crumble into saffron spice
While mellow mustard radiates
Solar stone of golden glow
Burning onto withered sunflowers
As the petals fall like flickering flames
Amber turns to ash
Burnout

White paint

Bleached bathrooms and tiles
Ceramics for the whole-hearted
Reflecting daylight
Fresh magnolia laundry on the line
Quiver into daisy chains
Fluffy florets of clouds float above
Counting sheep before you sleep
Slumped on your minimal chair
Pills and paper without shadow
A blissful delight
White paint purifies the sky
Spilling light into your life

3. ESCAPISM

Utopia

I want a pink house on the seventh street
Tiled floors, feeling the heat sizzling under bare feet
Aqua, iridescent luminous pool and beach-ball balloon
A Barbie doll's dream
Light rays ripple into a turquoise water dance
A blue portal to a fantasy island
Sip fresh-mint leaf mojitos and wiggle painted toenails
My villa, Spyreila
Bougainvillea crawling up the wall
Pink paradise in bloom
Life's a beach

4. Resilience and Recovery
(survival, strength, self-love, healing)

4. RESILIENCE AND RECOVERY

Bruises

Purple discolouration
Bleeding cranberry sauce
A pleasant distress
Clotting into hot black tar
Sticky enough to stretch the high roads
A break away from all the damage in your car
Inflated tyres for the pointless journey
Deflated

Barbara

Hot-dipped twisted steel wrapped around her waist
Clenching her teeth and ready for war
A commander of the force, navigating her way through a bloody-barbed obstacle, grinding to a halt at razors edge
Not even cutters can cut that
Night-time falls and pain stake, stabbing sensation in the uterus an enemy now a friend
Fed up with listening to Barbara Ann by the
Beach Boys on repeat, anything to numb the pain, water bottles for the heat
Endometriosis is a warzone, a battle that cannot be won
A disaster

Instinct

As Gazelle awakes
Nimble silhouette in the blood orange sunrise
She prepares for the fleet of her life
Hunted by a primal appetite

Lion is starved of sensual desire
A wildfire in his heart
He must adapt power and pace
But only one can pursue this race

He observes in grassland
Filmy Gazelle looks at him with her doey wide eyes
Fragile beauty and slender limbs
Welcomes him to her habitat

Lion lured in confusion
She does not run but stays
Threatened pride at a close distance
Game on

Her strength succeeds
He does not want a bite of raw meat
And the predator is now prey
Both are left in limbo

4. RESILIENCE AND RECOVERY

Oh, how I hate your guts

Oh, how I *detest* your guts
When you give me a sour kiss
And I am left with a bitter-sweet taste in my mouth

Spitting venom from your lips
My intestines coil into the form of a serpent
Forced to digest this infection
Prey on me vicious reptile

I swallow this poison
You feed me through your teeth
Don't bite your tongue
It is a distasteful diet

My love juices churn in my pit
Preparing to break down the toxins
A crushing hiss
Your words are pushed deeper into my tract
Oh, pitiful anger, how can I stomach this?

I am paralysed by this process
Recoiled, bursting at the seams
Stomach leaps like the serpent catching its prey
Hemotoxins explode into my stream
I return to bite

Oh, how I hate your guts
When you're spewing word vomit
I am gagging from that love-sick stench
As I return my attack
Choking from that acidic spike
Don't hold back

I have a gut feeling that this love sickness still lingers inside of me
Tongue-tied, eye-watering envy
A cyclic storm
When all I know is that I want to be free
I hate you with all my guts

Evelyn

She stumbles through the sleepy night
Rapidly breathing, as her toes curl in her shoes
Blessed with such escapism
Away from unbroken beatings
'You need knocking down a peg or two'
And he did, malleting her with such force
She fell to the floor like smashed porcelain
With her heavy-duty heart.
'Don't run away from me'
And so, she did, darted through the pitchy trees
Each branch is a silhouette of slender man
Snipped by thorny hands
Ripped tights and grazed knees
Deep-red drops of blood ooze into velvety blooms
Evelyn, the wilted rose
Lies there in a botanical bed of nettles
That stings more than the tears that run down her face
Evolution.

Departure

Come and go
The same old jokes leap into the air
And all that is left is a memory of a past person or event
As seasons change
There through the winter to keep you sheltered
Disappear into the spring to bloom and blossom
Leave behind the dead bark and the crusty leaves
Trodden by boots that walk for miles
Mother Nature will look after herself

Photosynthesis

Dead plants no longer need watering
To care for rise and revival
Nourish with water, soil, and refracted sunlight
Bright enough to burst into ripe and tender buds
Away from sap-sucking pests
That devour life of each leading leaf
As toothsome treats
Slow growth from a dried-out thief
There is enough oxygen to breathe

Body bag

All hung up like a punchbag
As energy seeps into sweat and chains
Transfer trauma from the brain
Through the zipped lining of bloodthirsty leather
Crouch and whimper away
Beyond our limits of pain
Fists as tight as your wallet
Wrapped wrists and blistered knuckles
Champion beast that jabs and hooks
Cruel feelings will bruise
Pressure drips unable to catch a breath
Snarling through gummy teeth
Better than drooling over a loser like you
The power is in my hands now

SAD (Seasonal Affective Disorder)

Hunched, heavy-lidded head
Tarnished and rugged weather
The body is worn, weak and thinner
These hours are the longest
Dragging the body out of bed

Uncombed frail branches
Hair falls out like stale leaves
Laid bare across the sheet
An emptiness to breathe

Damaged roots and shredded bark
Peeling layers and layers of flesh
Bedraggled and limp by storms
Saturated from all the tears shed
Cellular death

Stolen light creates a wilted thief
No aurora to fulfil the needs
Hibernate for another year
Hopeless beyond belief

Winter blues
Dimmed into moonlight
Luminous call
Spring is around the corner
Time to feel reborn

Asbestosis

Inflated airbags filled with shimmering shards and
  foggy fibres
The deadliest microscopic dreams
Scarred lungs will only heal quicker
When inhaling winter's death and exhaling summer's
  breath
Webbed with glassy wool in spectrums of light
Crystal formations defrost, glittering into dewy water
  droplets
Wheezy chest uncaged, as the spider flees to rest
Everything feels whole again

Bird brains

Crows and pigeons flock to the last of the crumbs
Large-beaked squawking mob
Pecking order to fight for survival
Beaded eyes of corruption and laced liquor
We are wingless birds in flight mode
Clipped freedom in a feathery fate
Crow calling at the cemetery
Funeral for the late beloved
Midnight omen

Black cat

Mysterious person asked me for a drink
And the next minute you know we are fucking
Whisked away for a midnight stay
Just a stray cat
Crawling the floors for food and affection
Eyes cut into gilded gemstones
Slipping into alleyways against fear and time
Rusting in the morning light
Shape-shifter

Watchers

The sun flickers through the Venetian blinds
We sip on our teas and watch the end of the world go by in chaos
Cigarette ends to build a bird's nest
Cancerous home for a fledglings' freedom
A comfortable ignorance
Safe and quiet inside
Bliss

Shedding

New skin to be formed
Scales versatile from sandstorms
That catch grit in your eyes
Watery-eyed mess
A hazy view

Nightfall

As soon as the sun goes down
The evening brings out the darkness that we veil
    throughout the daytime
Night walkers run riot
We are afraid of fear

Protection

Walk this journey alone
In old, cold bones
Put on your coat
The only love that keeps you warm
Long sleeves
That hug you through the storms

Antidote

Poetry is the purest medicine
Words that can be swallowed whole
Deep into the tract of fleshy tissue and soul
Digested to soothe, and ease aches
A remedy for disease
Tease out any tension
You will be lost for words

Maintenance

Our bodies are like machines
They require servicing
The tools to fix our problems and pain
Rusty parts and muscles grind against the bone
Internal pipes are filled with dust and grime
To be cleaned and cleansed for a purer life
Safety

Healer

I want to heal all the broken people
The constant suffering
A power from the heart and hand
To evaporate existential anxieties and the passing of time
Slow it all down, hold it in the tick of a moment
Before it all catches up and turns to dust
This is *our* purpose
To help and to heal

Breathalysed

Tipple on the tip of your tongue
Brewed breath stumbling over words
Energy stealers
I can no longer help you

Healing

Glugging
Water trickles through the veins
A refreshing sensation
Sun warming the roots of my hair
We can bleach it another time
Alone but in peace
I am breathing, soothed all at once
Waterfalls sound like the summer plunge
A dewy glow on the skin
Revitalised for an adventurous season
Cleansed and cleaned from capitalism

5. Cosmic and Existential Reflections
(celestial, universe, existentialism, mortality)

Blue kaleidoscope

Iris dazzles
In scattered sunlight
Infused by sharded illusions
Jewelled layers of amazonite
Mirrored in an everchanging view

Blinking beauty
Greenish-blue essence
Reflections of congruent crystals
Art Deco decadence
Fragmented dreams and desires

5. COSMIC AND EXISTENTIAL REFLECTIONS

Obsidian pupils pulsate
An optical mass
Asteroids shower
Into the formations of sea glass
A blue universe is created

Galaxies of gems
Clustered sights eternally restless
In space and time
The scope is endless
Infinite

White feathers

They say that white feathers are a gift from God
Dog is God spelt backwards
A heavenly message
The one who we lost

Soft, white feather
Silently sways to the ground
And lays in curled innocence
Ready to be patted and loved

Is this the fallen angel?
A sudden gusty breeze
Feather caught under my feet
Wagging in the wind, to make-believe

Seasons change with this delicate snow
Blanketing the earth in a pearly glow
Gifted with celestial presence
Now it's my dog's time to go

Shades of blue

Plunge into the pool of blue
As the water droplets fall from your eye
These are the deepest of fears

In cold ultramarine light
Wade into violet waves
Of infinite harmony and bliss

A distance so close to touch
Draw a breath with your cobalt crayon
In a powdered existence

Indigo bleeds
Flooding ultra-cool
Cascading into copper sulphate flow

Submerge
Sink deeper
Drown
Become blue
You are the coolest

Sun and moon

Retreat into the sun
A perfect sphere of light
Blended into the night
Of moonlight and ultra-violet rays
It's a lunar phase
Fade away

5. COSMIC AND EXISTENTIAL REFLECTIONS

Mission

Floating in voids
Lost but going somewhere
A grain against the pain
Of collided rocks and screens
Hide behind the sheet, never to be seen
Meteorites seem closer to breaking the Earth apart
Just like the craters in our hearts
That are imprinted on the moon's surface
Pounded dust by the astronauts' boots
The magnetic field is wide enough to run
In Earth's orbit of the sun
Disintegrate into the lunar soil
Pinched in the silhouette of moonlight
Cool white and warm yellow
Foundations

Watchdog

I was visited by my canine friend
It was too real to be a dream
A being of intense light
Wreathed in a halo glow
In the presence of adolescence
Healthy, young, and boundless paws
Wiry fur and lolling tongue
Rolling into an orb through grassy fields and daisy
    heads
Realm became a reality
Our human-animal consciousness burns bright enough
To cleanse and purify bad energies
My lost dog has found me
Watchful guardian and protector of pain
Let's walk together through eternity and rain

Presence

I feel like everything is ending and beginning at the same time

Past, present, and future intertwined

Deep in the oblivion of energy

The protagonist

There is comfort in magnifying people and places
   around you
At first, everything is an overstimulation –
An explosion of shapes, colours and sounds
You take the time to reflect – how do you belong in
   this worldly bubble?
Creating stories and impressions of individuals in your
   head
An editor
Particularly through the filmy train windows
Passing moments to one destination
And the show must go on

Burnt toast

The morning leaves a stale taste
Crunchy bites with coffee grains
Daylight and dust filter through the windowpane
Zone out from all responsibilities for a day
Scrape the charcoaled layer with a buttered knife
Eat all your crusts that border your freedom
Wholemeal bread is your world

Dust

Particles under microscopic inspection
Drifting through every worthless hour
In a home that you putrefy in
And the cell walls are made of your dead flesh
Choked by the fear of being watched
Polluted prison

5. COSMIC AND EXISTENTIAL REFLECTIONS

Crisis

Society   Mental Health
Capitalism
             RentMortgage
Age Sex Relationships
Retirement

Death   Existence

   Dreams   Rejection

                   Loneliness

                       Emptiness
                              Dissociation

Disappear

Possessed

It feels like someone is wringing a flannel, draining through every neuron
I am a lost person
This numbness and intangible rage are dominating my thoughts which I once had in control
I feel possessed, even *they* said I woke up one night, wide-eyed and muttering in a sleep-paralysis state
Where do I go now?
I ponder a lot about death
My deepest fear is death
The world, which was once my odyssey, is now my enemy

Humans

What does it mean to be valued?
Is a value a profit or a principle?
To assess and estimate everything
Our morals become one
If you remove that number, do you then become numb?
Work your system that is weaved into the heart's chambers
As knots in your stomach are ready to be loosened
Walking the tightrope to your destination of free will
Away from exploitation and trade
Mastering the power of authenticity
This is our true reality

Rat race

Early morning rise
For the experimental grind
Another day encircling the wheel just to survive
Cold-blooded and energy-deprived
Nibbling at the stale scraps
Laid out on the yellow brick road to our destination
   and freedom
Scurry and scutter
Always in a rush to be productive
Repeat daily routine
Entrapment

Eleven lines

Writing lines
Yellow lines
Power lines
Straight lines
Fine lines
White lines
Snorting lines
Blurred lines
Help lines
Life line
Train line

Timewaster

Worn out of hope and minutes
In all those careless hours that you devour
Clockwise to your playtime
Pending doom driven by springs
One day you will be the grandfather clock
As the pendulum swings
Unable to handle the time that you have wasted
When the body stops
It's never too late to be on time for death

Retirement

Dewy youth that sits deliciously on the lips
Moisture collects in the flower head
Fragrant beauty and naivety
Blushed innocence to maturity

As the petals shrivel and brown
Wrinkled tan in sunlight
Skin taught and bone dry
To eternal sleep in the ground

Apocalypse

Part I: Black Rabbit

Solitude away from warrens
Networks that belong to the servant of hearts
Glossy jet black to chestnut brown hare
Garden party for one
Territorial behaviour
Digging and foraging for treasures
The grass isn't greener on the other side
Grey clouds drift over
Shape-shifting pareidolia
Ears pointing that way on alert for danger
Pigmented fur surfaces a midnight haze
Nature's call for help

5. COSMIC AND EXISTENTIAL REFLECTIONS

Part II: Black Sun

Shade blocks the sphere
As summer rots to crisp
Apocalypse blankets the earth
Rabbit on the run
Coddled cottontail under threat
Climate in cinders
Sooty fur, and thinning strands
Hairless ball to hold
Curled in the palm of human hands
Beady eyes sink into sticky mucus
Crescent pupils evolve an eclipse
Light in life falls to darkness in dust
Malt, ash, and crust
Disintegrate

Part III: Blood Moon

The Moon is on fire
Pooling into vermillion liquid
Skywatchers draw their last breath
Scattered flakes of fleshy red
Flicker from ruby to crimson rust
Outlining constellations of figures and animals
The last roamers
Crackled misery vapourised
The shadow of earth is a blackout
A veil of darkness
Total eclipse
Terminus

5. COSMIC AND EXISTENTIAL REFLECTIONS

Sheep

As the train shuttles by the dusky fields
A sheep lies dead in decay, detached in a woollen cloud
A reminder of our innocence and time
A corpse

Reconcile

Dusky evening
Snag the sun in your hands
Implant it into your chest and feel the flames detonate within
Know it is okay to let go
Don't be afraid, you will be the new energy on the run
Go now, jump
Take a deep breath and fall with grace
To the heartbeats of our last race
The last colours you will see
Yellow, blue, and black
Flickering through the blinds all too quickly
Movie scenes
Marks on a painting

Hair

Consuming your evening meal
Spaghetti wraps around your fork
An intimate and delightful moment of dopamine
Until you find yourself swallowing a strand of hair
Pulling it from the throat as a loose thread on a needle
Your meal soon becomes unpleasant
Detached from the body
Loss of self and other

Dead hair rapidly grows around you
It falls into your food
It sticks to your clothes
It blocks the plug hole as you shower
It prickles on your legs that you shaved only yesterday
It appears in places unknown
One, two, three on the chin
An overgrown repulsion

6. *Human Connections*
(lust, infatuation, modern life)

Milk

White liquid emulsion rolls down the thighs
Satin glaze in sunlight to a pasteurised mess
Semi-skimmed silk sheets wrapped around our feet
Milking me for everything worth
Condensed sweetness, creamy and consumed whole
Canned notions in pints half-full
Lactation from the breast, a sensation to feed you best
Tolerant to your lactose intolerance
Acidic sour taste
Expired

Lava

Sex and cigarettes
Volcanic ash and smoke on your lips
Embraced for this eruption
Magma liquid flows through your lustful veins
Heat and fire bond us together
As you steal my oxygen
Solidifying in the coolness of those Scottish-sea algae
   eyes
Frozen in time

Nectar

Take a large gulp and swallow slimy larvae
Feed the stomach starved of lust
Fluttery cocoon evolves into the butterfly experience
Complete metamorphosis
Delicate wings unfold into instruments of symmetrical
    shapes and colour
Camouflaged in excitement, dread, and fear
Light electric euphoria
Love is a choice with action
But butterflies will fly away
Once you are safe and secure
The truth is fading
Reproduction

Vibrations

Dance the night away into techno dreams
Glancing as your cyan eyes flash under strobe lights
Feel the electric beat race into goosebumps
Hearts are hungry and mouths are thirsty
With witnesses to watch us drop
Falling as we move together in time
Enigmatic energy
Encapsulated in bodily expression
To make believe through a filmy club scene
Melt into the morning hours
Expired memories

Judgement

Painted on the ceiling of the Sistine Chapel
An exhibition where no one can photograph you
A work of art sculpted with a drawn eye
That tones the Renaissance figure
Of creator and creation in classical expression
Carved by the compliments received
Bronze torso with marbled skin
Shrine to your robust body
Fresh nude paste turns to dusty fresco
Descend to your fate
Fragile plaster crumbles in lust
You can't preserve an ego
Mankind can be unkind

Long distance

Soulful fires
Burning miles away
Travel through the optic nerve
Into the ozone layers of pupils
Obsession and passion
Laughing until we dance the fire out
As silhouettes tremor in the soot and smoke
Too broke to fix our hearts
You make me safe and independent
Chemistry is Alchemy
That co-exists in a lifetime of compatibility
Conflict in our values and goals
That roar in the fiery Lion's mane
Golden Syrup for heated breath and breakfast eyes
I see you swallow the day in two
Distant winners pursuing the same fight
With fear, scars, and open wounds
Cutting through the air that lingers with haunted voices
Intensity

6. HUMAN CONNECTIONS

Fierce sex and love intertwined
Our cords are cut short
With the red wine I drank
Blurry eyes and speechless surprises
Your eyes devour all mine
As we deliver small glances at one another
Dance through the day
We are just normal people wanting normal things
Uncommunicative of true feelings
I crave you for my self-esteem
An attraction mirrored in shattered souls
Twists of fate made by the high priestess itself
Fake friends when we are truly lovers
You say you don't like needy
But you need me

Grit

Caught under your spell
Bronzed waves and grey eyes
Box to the beat in silk shorts
Cool-hearted infatuation in gains
Sail free, cocktails and sand grains under our feet
Before Sandman removes your eyes
Sprinkle dust before dawn
Gritty teeth and sleep
For better dreams and fantasies
Suffering

Honeymoon

It started like a summer breeze
Circulating through the green trees
Pumping oxygen into the bloodstream
That flooded raspberry sauce on bitter ice cream
But we fell into a pool of murky water
Drowning, unable to breathe
As the birds migrate, the temperature cools
Change of season, the leaves turn a crusty brown
A stale and tedious disease
That spreads to grow thicker fur
Matted in the gum that stuck us together
Hardened the heart of fire into cinder paste
Debris that can't reignite
Love has gone to waste

Denim eyes

Levi looks effortlessly cool in those jeans
Dip-dyed, frayed cotton mess
Stylised in my size
A perfect fit with no label yet
But I'd dye for you
Weep and weft, just hanging on by a thread
Drenched in indigo tears

Hunger

What is it like to be loved rather than lusted?
Are the differences deceptive?
To fuck before we love
It is a selfish need

Mariner

I don't want mediocre.
Your boring words made me write another poem
For a better conversation with myself – at least it flows
I see that you are sober now
After your little love-drunk tease
You knew exactly what the plan was to please me
Emptied the bottle dry
Did it give you clarity?
It must have been too easy for you to see clearly
Back to your senses
Although already aware of your prosperity
I cracked your bottle now
Fragments

Storyteller

The scent of us on your sheets
Lies
The meals that we made
Lies
The deepest philosophical conversations
Lies
The promise to commit
Lies
The open communication
Lies
The intimacy and grasp of my thighs
Lies
The flowers that you buy
Lies
Stale, crusty, yellow leaves
I hope you die soon

Sluggish

Slug in the drudgery
Slugging along to work
Leaving a silvery, slippery trail behind
Suppressed but still shining bright

No backbone, just a vertebrate
Don't break your back for the nine-to-five
You have no spine anyway
Spineless mollusc

Red carpet

Arriving at the grand debut for all the world to pick
   apart their vulnerabilities
Left chambered in a garden of endangered
   rhododendrons
Clustered and fruitful, confetti for the celebrity
Red carpet trodden by worn-out boots and babies'
   shoes
Crushed daydreams, desires and even failures
Plushy crimson luxury
Hollywood première
An exquisite entrance for the ones who lose

Instagram

Double tap, red hearts, 10+ new direct messages
And 4 new messages from the same old 'friend'
Everyone wants instant replies, consuming all your time
Emotionally drained and one step behind
It never ends

Getting lost in the reel world based on algorithms and likes
Editing your photographs to make them look nice
An overwhelming urge to keep up with the trends
Validation from the orbiters who watch your stories but never want to talk
Let them view your best life, the silent stalkers

Online dating

Jump into the dating cesspool, relax and play it cool:
'I'm looking for intimacy without commitment'
'Open to kids though'
'Swipe right if you want to have some fun'
'I'm hoping you don't take yourself too seriously'
'I know the best spot in town for wine and pizza'
Countless options

Orbiting

Orbit around the sun and earth
Fuzzy head
Watching over me
Through detonated media screens

I feel you breathing over me
Even though you are distantly far away
You encircle me tirelessly
Until my head hurts

6. HUMAN CONNECTIONS

Commoners

The neighbourhood watch is just for individuals who
    want to be celebrities
Creating 'protected' communities on patrol to seek
    crime against humanity
Perhaps 'busybodies', bursting their bubbles seems a
    safer space to me…

The Gardener
Doris is preening her plants for the annual Garden of
    the Year competition
While May's garden down the road is blooming with
    hyacinths, daffodils, and tulips
A colourful coronation for a prized delight
As soon as the evening arrives, Doris is planning to
    pour weedkiller and snip the stems with her shears.
May Doris be this year's winner

The Curtain-twitcher
Brenda always has her curtains closed
Though, sometimes the curtain folds, inviting a streak of sunlight
Out of the shadows, the vampire is caught peeking through the slit
Gaunt, and bloodthirsty
Hunting for her next meal of the night

The Driveway Guard
Mick prefers to play the cards right
One who lets his guard down
Leaning against the fence, looking to make an enemy as a friend
Interrupting the peace of passers-by
Inviting people in for tea, reminiscing about the past
You won't be the last one

Bike Thief
Anonymous identity, but has been spotted in a balaclava and leather gloves
A bike chain of events leads to missing alloy wheels
Trails of oil stains and burnt rubber rims
A penny farthing will cost you
Vengeance is waiting

6. HUMAN CONNECTIONS

Facebook Drama Queen
Stacey wants the world to know that a cat has bitten her toe
Checking into the hospital for infection
Updating her location on Facebook
A pity party of commenters for show

Nightshifter
Nigel is a werewolf, he sleeps through the day and wakes at night
On call for another shift, groggy, sleepy-eyed, and growling canines
Scrape and de-ice the frost from the car window
For he is the one who lives in cold blood
The true colours of crime under street and moonlight

Celebrities

What does it mean to be a celebrity?
To sell your body and soul
Visible to the world and harassed by internet trolls
Hypnotised followers
We all look to tally validation and monetary gain
Enough plastic is pumped into the body and bank
    account
Egotistical, only time will tell if vanity remains
What happened to our brains?
Sucked into scrolling and laughing our lives away
Hiding behind our broken bodies and pay
We are comfortable staying insane

Washing machine

40 degrees rinse of your rotting clothes
Sanitised cycle for cleanliness
Liquid detergent makes your shit smell nice for a little
    while
Wash, dry, hang and wear
Until we repeat the same cycle again
The fragile garments were spun with no time and love,
    for hand-wash only care
Soapy displacement

Circus

Ringmaster directs and whips the juggling multi-tasker
A class act for treating people like clowns
Our costumes are now everyday clothes
Laughing stock at the tears painted down our faces
We are the performers in the clown show
Entertainment is painful

7. *The Darkest Hours*

At night-time, the darkness awakens our most intrusive and irrational thoughts.

Dilemmas

Go with the flow
One that is putrid and poisoned
Rotting the body to near-death
Disrupting an explosion in your head
Tooth erupted through the gummy sponge
As the bones bury in their bed
Where is the wisdom now?
Exercise sewn through muscle tissues
To injure and repair
Slashed wrists and scored arms
Every time I think about roping my neck
The threads fray one by one
Until you're left with the last strand
Without a partner to grip my hand

7. THE DARKEST HOURS

On the verge of losing your job
Dissociation is a recession
To be made redundant from this lifetime
Don't blame the universe for your problems
This is human nature
Alone and cold
Our fault
Fall into a black hole
Despair

Electricity

The soul hurts
It needs sun on the skin
To illuminate the cold and dark home inside
A power cut into cords, the earth wire is fed to feel
　　alive again
Wrapped into the wrists and neck
A fashion item called a choker
Energy saver
Lifesaver

Hypochondriac

The clock is ticking
Tick, tick, tick
The cyst is growing
5, 10, 15 cm
The egg will crack
Yellow monster suffocating in white linen
My erratic mind is on crack
Let it leak irrational thoughts
Before the brain is scrambled
For eggs on toast

Fear and hope

Although I am very afraid of death, there is peace in knowing that it will all be over one day
The vacuum of blankness, the unknown or to reincarnate into a new life form
But in that same blip, it makes you appreciate the feel-good moments
Every glistening line wrinkled under the eye
The shimmers on the water's surface that keep you afloat under sunset

Quick fix

Drinking alone again
Wine or an IPA every day
The liver is scarred
Crying on the floor again
Another problem, another thing turned to shit
Trying to fix all the holes in your wall
With all-purpose filler
The only purpose you have, leaving you dry and unfulfilled
Perhaps you can use that drill in the side of your head
So, the information is chipped here instead
Rather than a tin can of chemicals and cancer rotting your existence
Enhance your delusions
The solution for a fulfilled life

Familiarity

Feeling frustrated, and stuck in a rut
It's like swimming in a stagnant lake
Infested with parasites

Shit out of luck

Look towards the future they say
Instead, you're just looking at the same four cream walls
Now feeling sorry for yourself
Problem after problem
Day in, day out

Trying anything just to fill that void
The comfort zone becomes uncomfortable and airless
Paint the walls a brighter colour
A shade to not be afraid and bring change

Does anyone really know where they are going; after all, what is the point in knowing?

7. THE DARKEST HOURS

Suicidal conversations

Why do humans bring suffering and conflict to one another and animals?
I believe I am not made for this world
I don't want to work until I am old
I don't want to work full-time
Why are we slaves to the system?
Why is *everything* about money?
I don't feel real
I am crazy
I feel empty
I aborted my baby
I want to drive my car off the bridge
I want to rope my neck
But I don't want to live or die either
I will be forever alone
I will go to hell
I haven't met the 'one'
I won't be able to have kids now
I need help but they think I am attention-seeking

So selfish
It could be worse
At least you are 'alive'
Nobody cares, nobody helps, you are left to your fate anyway

We can only be *strong* for so long

Conclusion

I want to reflect and express the rawness of becoming 29 – the last year in my 20s.

Today we live in a superficial world comparing our lives with each other, obsessing over celebrities and materialism, chasing our youth instead of accepting ageing (and yes, I am a victim to all of this, most of us are). I mean we all love escapism, wealth, having nice things, exploring the world, and no one really wants to get old, but death is inevitable, and we have to accept that we change with time.

We torture ourselves if we aren't meeting a goal, or gaining a certain thing by a certain milestone, under the pressure gauge of societal expectations and social media influences. Life is hard though, and whoever passes by and says it is easy is lying to themselves. We are on a wheel of fortune and for some people they just get lucky, and for others their worlds are vastly declining. I do believe this is a part of why we are struggling as a generation. It feels like our worth is constantly defined by productivity and 'numbers' as a value.

Everyone's circumstances and timelines are different. In a positive light though, and as a woman, I feel privileged to have the freedom of choice now, to shape life, and to work on my timeline against the pressures in this generation.

I have been learning that health, hobbies, experiences and personal relationships are more important than climbing to the top of the corporate ladder. Happiness is internal, more like a mindset that we can try to nurture, in many ways; one that isn't 100 per cent reliant on money (even though, of course, it does help). However, happiness factors into our environments and impacts our growth and feelings: to leap out of our comfort zones, to take risks, to feel the sun on your skin, to surround yourself with healthy people, animals and nature, to be present, humble, enjoy the experiences, whilst trying not to worry about what the future holds. The future is out of our control, and our journeys don't always align with our dreams. Some of us may just seek peace and simplicity instead. While we can't dictate the course of our lives, we can guide the sail through the choppy and rough waters, finding calmness in between. So, for now, all we can do is manage the present situation as best we can, knowing that this uncertainty will pass and eventually flow.

I have also been learning to set boundaries and focus on the things that bring peace and joy and the people that add greatness to my life. Let people go who are out for their gain, those you can no longer relate to, or waste your time, as time is our true value here. Your time and health are sanctities, and anything can change at any moment. *No one is safe.* At least we can try, open our minds and follow our gut instincts.

Life is trying to find a balance or make our way through a maze and acceptance is the key. Express your flaws, your strengths, your pain and your pleasures as this is what it is to be human. This is what it is like to live through light and shade – the shadows of our lives.

PAPER SHADOWS

www.ingramcontent.com/pod-product-compliance
Lightning Source LLC
LaVergne TN
LVHW041638060526
838200LV00040B/1626